A Review of the Book

THE CASE FOR TRUMP

by Victor Davis Hanson

Review by **FREDY BURGOS**
Project Director, Americans for a Conservative Agenda

Introduction by **HON. VANCE WILKINS**
Former Speaker of the Virginia House of Delegates

***Review of* The Case for Trump *by Victor Davis Hanson*,** is published by FreedomPublishers.com for Americans for a Conservative Agenda.

This is a Review, not the full 392-page book. Freedom Publishers is not associated with Victor Davis Hanson or the publisher of his book, which we recommend and which can be purchased at FreedomPublishers.com, Amazon.com or your local bookstore.

Book Review and Afterword by Fredy Burgos, Project Director and Co-Founder, Americans for a Conservative Agenda (formerly Americans for the Trump Agenda)

Introduction by Hon. Vance Wilkins, Former Speaker of the Virginia House of Delegates

Special thanks to the following who have made the publishing of this review possible:

Associate Editor: Owen Jones

Executive Editor: Hanover Henry

Cover design and typesetting: Spencer Grahl

Amanda G. Hyland, Esq.
Taylor, English, Duma LLP, Atlanta, Georgia

This publication was made possible thanks to a grant from the Freedom Center Foundation.

This pocketbook and the organizations which have worked together to publish and circulate it do not advocate for or against candidates for local, state or federal office. Along with the author of *The Case for Trump*, we are fans of former President Trump and strongly advocate for his agenda.

Copyright© July 2020, First Edition
Copyright© June 2021, Second Edition

Donations to pay for more copies of this pocketbook to be printed and distributed may be made to:

Americans for a Conservative Agenda
(formerly Americans for the Trump Agenda)
A project of United States Public Policy Council,
a 501/c/4 public policy corporation.
Donations not tax deductible.

TrumpYes.org

or mail

Americans for a Conservative Agenda
Freedom Center, P.O. Box 820,
Stuarts Draft, VA 24477-0820.

or

Freedom Center Foundation
Chairman@FreedomCenterFoundation.org

Gifts to the Foundation are tax deductible on your federal tax return. Gifts of $1000 or more only please. Recognized by IRS as a 501(c)3 charity.

Additional copies of this pocketbook may be ordered for a gift of $5 each, 3 for $10, 10 for $20, 100 for $150 plus postage and handling of $3 plus 10%.
Inquire for larger orders.

FreedomPublishers.org for online orders & other books and pocketbooks including the hardcover "The Case for Trump" book by Victor Davis Hanson.

INTRODUCTION

By Vance Wilkins
Former Speaker of the Virginia House of Delegates

REACTIONS TO THE Presidency of Donald Trump are rarely neutral. They tend to be either enthusiastic or unabated hatred.

This review of Victor Davis Hanson's book lays out the facts, proving that the Trump Presidency was about accomplishment. He actually kept the promises he made to the American people.

Trump made America great again by any standard of measurement, as we show here. There is no question that the Presidency of Joseph Biden represents a giant step backwards.

A REVIEW OF THE BOOK *THE CASE FOR TRUMP*

The revisionism we face today from the White House, Senate, House, major media and liberal-left Big Tech social media, are all based upon emotional hate, not facts.

In my view, any fair-minded American who reads *Review of the Case for Trump*, will become like us, a fan of Donald Trump.

What is at stake is first, whether our country will allow liberals to completely "cancel" the accomplishments of former President Trump, and second, whether Trump followers win back the House and Senate in 2022 and the White House in 2024—with perhaps a return by Trump himself as our President.

On behalf of Americans for a Conservative Agenda (formerly Americans for the Trump Agenda) and their *Trump Yes* effort, we believe you'll find this pocketbook useful in presenting your case for Trump.

A PERSONAL NOTE

by Fredy Burgos

*Project Director, Americans for a Conservative Agenda
(formerly Americans for the Trump Agenda)
and author of this book review*

THE ONSLAUGHT OF ATTACKS against President Donald Trump from 2016 through the election of 2020 were unprecedented in American history. They continue today. As a strong and longstanding Trump supporter, I find that they are overwhelming at times, vicious and so often, highly personal in attacking not only Trump but also his supporters.

Often, such attacks, including personal conversations with some friends, relatives, neighbors, co-workers, repeated lies and emotional hate rather than actual facts.

Thankfully, this paperback, revised from our first printing and distribution in 2020, gives all of us Trump fans, a tool to help "make the case" for Donald Trump.

We believe that the vilification of former President Trump by the liberal-left, their mainstream media allies, and the liberal-left dominated Big Tech giants is not just wrong factually, but is also downright evil.

They go far beyond simply disagreeing with Trump. They are vicious and evil in their tactics. That's why Edmund Burke, a Member of Parliament of Great Britain, courageously sided with the American revolutionaries, saying, "The only thing necessary for the triumph of evil, is that good men do nothing."

Former President Trump consistently demonstrates faith in the goodness of his supporters. Now we have a simple pocketbook to share with others, which shows why we believe in his goodness.

I hope you will use the information provided in this extended review of *The Case for Trump*, and will help us get the word out about what you learn in his pocketbook.

Please consider how you can help. You can order more copies of this paperback. Donate to Americans for a Conservative Agenda to help us give out more of them. Buy the terrific book by Victor Davis Hanson.

I hope you will find this handy pocketbook useful to helping you defend the Trump Agenda.

THEME 1

TRUMP AS TRAGIC HERO

The last thing I expected to learn from classical scholar Hanson is that Donald Trump is not a unique figure in history by any means. Hanson draws on his extensive knowledge of classical and modern political and literary history to make his case that Donald Trump has many renowned antecedents.

Consider Sophocles' tragic hero Ajax. According to Hanson, "Ajax's soliloquies about a rigged system and the lack of recognition accorded his undeniable accomplishments is Trumpian to the core." Achilles is an outlier from Thessaly.

He is pitted against mediocre deep state leaders Menelaus and "the overrated careerist King Agamemnon."

Likewise, the "fake news" media would give no credit for Trump's accomplishments, including a thawing of relations with North Korea, stellar economic results, or criminal justice reform, to name just a few.

Tragic heroes do not fit in with their times. Personal loyalty, not civic duty, is their creed. And Donald Trump was the most loyal President to his supporters that we have ever witnessed.

Hanson points out that The Magnificent Seven are not the stuff of school boards and city hall. As with all tragic heroes, Trump—in office and out—is a sacrificial victim. Even now, he's willing to take the barbs and arrows from the angry left that have been directed at you and me for decades.

Trump is willing to sacrifice his wealth and honor on behalf of his "tribe: the forgotten Americans."

Trump knows that winning is sufficient reward for all of the unfair criticism he receives.

"If one wants to win a war," says Hanson, "then one looks for people like the off-putting, cigar chomping General Curtis LeMay and his thunderous B-29's to win it."

The left sees General LeMay as a brutal war monger. Those of us who are patriots with common sense see him as someone who did what it takes to win a war against a merciless enemy.

Hanson reminds us that the tragic hero knows that he will be ostracized by the civilization he is working to protect. "Dirty Harry could not be the public face of the San

Francisco Police Department any more than Trump could appear presidential in the same manner as Obama."

How many snowflake lefties do you know who are fans of Dirty Harry?

"Ajax lived by an obsolete black-and-white code that is no longer compatible with the ascendant polis. Likewise, it is to be expected that Trump's blunt views would be mocked and resisted by Washington. John Creasy (played by Denzel Washington) knew that only he had the ability to deal with lethal cartel kidnappers and he did not flinch."

The question for Hanson, as it is for us, is not Trump's ability or desire to be "presidential," but "whether or not the frontier farmers had a solution apart from the gunslinger Shane."

Therefore, Hanson is not surprised that Trump failed to enjoy the honeymoon typically given to new presidents. It took two years for Trump to settle on a group of senior cabinet members who were both highly qualified—like Secretary of State Pompeo—and also personally loyal to the president and his vision.

Trump's critics raged that almost anyone could do a better job as president. Since these words were written, we have seen them proven out by the gaggle of half-baked, unqualified Democrat candidates who ran to replace Donald Trump, including a small city mayor, a gadfly billionaire, a New-Age guru, and, the inevitable establishment choice, a man who is obviously suffering from old-age dementia.

That man now, thanks to the nefarious efforts of the Radical Left, the Fake News liberal media, and liberal left Big Tech, now occupies the White House—the winner of a stolen election.

The Trump "paradox," as Hanson characterizes it, has resulted in Trump successfully fighting off Russia-gate, Ukraine-gate, two impeachments, and a relentless campaign to blame him for the COVID-10 pandemic. Having been foiled at every turn, Donald Trump's enemies were left with no option other than to outright steal the 2020 election from him.

Trump's ability to deflect and outwit his enemies remains as much a mystery to his progressive critics as it always had—and probably always will.

THEME 2

THE TRUMP AGENDA

THERE WERE MANY FACTORS creating the Trump phenomenon, but only he had the ability to see and speak for a large swath of forgotten voters, angry over their "accelerating decline." Trump told them that he believed in them and in America. They loved it. Still do.

The name Thucydides is not exactly the first word that rolls off your tongue when asked about Donald Trump. But Hanson has actually read Thucydides and believes the comparison is quite apt. Victor Davis Hanson is direct: "Trump is a modern-day Thucydides. He has the ability to understand true causes vs. pretexts, especially when it comes to our endless wars."

Trump's foreign policy has shown a vigor as well as "a common-sense acuity not seen in recent history." He never embarked on a presidential "apology tour." He was derided for calling the Korean dictator "little rocket man" and being "short and fat." But Trump understood that most of the world was predicated on "childish minds insulting one another." "Trump pursues a deliberate strategy of unpredictability that causes America's enemies to be more restrained."

According to Hanson, "Trump was willing to initiate trade wars to implement his signature agenda: overturning the post-war world economic order, especially regarding trade. Despite predictions of a global trade war and crashing economy, Trump's imposition of tariffs against China and Mexico, and the threat of EU tariffs resulted in a willingness to talk."

Trump jaw-boned U.S. companies into staying put or coming home. "Workers saw this for what it was: a genuine concern for their interest and the well-being of their families and communities." For the first time in many years real wages were rising.

Trump's promise to secure our borders and end illegal immigration was the most explosive part of his agenda and met with the most opposition, according to Hanson. The urban elites only know immigrants "as their maids and gardeners."

They don't know the poor blacks, Hispanics and whites who are deprived of a livelihood by illegal immigrants. Nor are they exposed to the crime and other social pathologies endemic to many illegal immigrant communities.

Trump pointed out the selfishness of the open border advocates. They either derived a political or economic benefit from illegal immigration. Trump had both the more logical argument and the better politics. But in the last analysis, no other candidate for President could have pulled it off.

The gist of Hanson's argument is this: "Trumpism is inseparable from Trump." It's unlikely that any other politician will ever be able to compare.

That said, officeholders and candidates who stand with Trump on his issues and who overlook his mannerisms, **do exceptionally well in primary and general elections**. Those who stand back from him or who do not identify with him, are not as able to overcome their opponent's attacks. This was evident from the 2018 off year election results and "down ballot" results in 2020, where pro-Trump Republicans gained seats —a fact overlooked by most pundits.

This is the fact that Trump's leftist critics cannot stand: "Trump the person transcends his ideas." If McCain or Romney were "aspirin," then Trump is "chemotherapy."

His supporters are willing to go through the toxic treatment in order to conquer the "disease." They defend his rhetoric because he is merely retaliating on their behalf against years of attacks on them as racists. And they love office holders and office seekers who stand with Trump, not at all because any of them mimic Trump the man, but because they follow Trump the advocate.

THEME 3

TRUMP ISN'T MR. ROGERS

But what about Trump's crudeness, you ask? Yah, I like what he's doing you might say, but I don't necessarily agree with how he expresses himself.

But Hanson is nothing if not an excellent historian, succinctly putting Trump's presidency in its proper perspective. "Had Presidents Wilson, FDR, JFK, and LBJ lived in the era of Facebook, Google, Twitter, cable news and cell phone cameras, they would all have been driven from office."

Their crudity, their sexual behavior, their hidden medical problems made

Trump's behavior while in the White House look positive by comparison. Nor would Eisenhower have been nominated had the media not covered for his extramarital affair with his Army chauffeur. With Trump there was not a hint of extramarital affairs in the White House.

No hidden medical problems. And his crude speech, both public and private, pales in comparison to the pathological crudity of LBJ.

We have to view Trump's public image in the context of unprecedented negative media coverage, which includes conservative "Never Trumpers." The conservative "Never Trumpers" claim Trump has forsaken the Reagan "high ground," while glossing over many of Reagan's own public statements.

Being given their own brand name by a very supportive national news media, many if not most of these members of the liberal-Democrat/"Anti-Trump" coalition only became fans of Ronald Reagan after he was long gone from office and didn't need their support.

As for the charge that Trump offended our allies while rejecting the sober advice of his foreign policy advisors, Truman repeatedly shocked: by dropping two atomic bombs over the objection of many in his cabinet, by recognizing Israel against the advice of most in his State Department, by offending his FDR holdovers by breaking from the Soviet Union and establishing a policy of containment.

The Pentagon opposed his desegregation of the military, and his national security advisers counseled against sending troops to save Korea. Historians have favorably judged his crassness as "plain speaking."

With access to Twitter, Truman would have outclassed Trump with a flurry of "ad hominem counter-attack outbursts" similar to the anti-Trump diatribes we see 24/7 on major media and social media.

Trump's "ungentlemanly" behavior must also be judged in the context of left-wing characterization of the Fort Hood massacre as "work-place violence," or renaming Islamic terrorism as a "man-caused disaster," or Hillary Clinton's slander that Trump supporters represent a "basket of deplorables."

Crudity does not begin to describe the reaction to Trump by the hysterical left. When Trump won, polls, conventional wisdom and political science were discredited. The response was not self-examination but collective fury.

Obscenity and threats of violence were used to demonize Trump—from celebrities to mainstream politicians. Chants of "kill him," "assassinate him," "hang him," "cut off his head," "punch him in the face," were met with laughter and applause.

A Bernie Sanders supporter shot at prominent Republicans playing baseball and gravely wounded Congressman Steve Scalise. Congresswoman Maxine Waters urged people to prevent cabinet members from eating in restaurants, telling them that "they're not welcome anymore, anywhere."

Hillary Clinton announced she was part of the "resistance" as if she were some courageous resistance fighter in Nazi occupied France where there was no longer any free speech and those captured were imprisoned, tortured and killed.

More ominously, Obama holdovers in Trump's administration began to organize resistance. Former Attorney General Loretta Lynch predicted that resistance to Trump requires not only marching but "the shedding of blood." Hillary Clinton announced that civility can only return once democrats are back in charge.

Never Trumper Mitt Romney blasted the Trump creed as "racism, misogyny, bigotry, xenophobia, vulgarity and, most recently, threats and violence." He called Trump a "phony," his promises "worthless." The man derided as a goody-two shoes by the mainstream liberal media when he ran for President was suddenly proclaimed as a great man of principle.

Never Trumpers encouraged a former CIA operative and Goldman Sachs banker to run as a third-party candidate with the hope that he, as a Mormon, would carry Utah and throw the election into the House of Representatives. Trump carried Utah by 18 points.

The Never Trump movement had no practical effect on election day, with Trump winning 90 percent of Republican voters, as good or better than any previous GOP nominee.

THEME 4

THE BLUE STATE NARRATIVE

The "blue state narrative," as Hanson terms it, is "condescending to everyone not living in coastal cities." It didn't hurt Trump's chances when Hillary Clinton characterized Trump supporters as "naïve, easily deceived, deplorable!"

Even after Trump was elected in 2016, the blue state narrative continued. Joe Biden called Trump voters "the dregs of society." Hillary Clinton sulked and whined and blamed everyone but her arrogant and detached campaign manner for her humiliating defeat.

Even FBI agents got in on the act. "Donald Trump was the first to counterpunch against this false narrative. Trump proved that populism can be a state of mind and not something pre-ordained by class."

THEME 5

TRUMP: MASTER SALESMAN

Trump's *Apprentice* viewers alone represented 18% of registered voters in the 2016 election. They saw him as someone who fired incompetents and rewarded the hard working and successful. His base voters did not want more "dignity" in their candidate. They wanted results.

The left loves to ridicule Trump as a loose cannon, but Hanson believes Trump chooses his targets and his epithets carefully when using them in public. As one columnist put it, "**The press takes him literally, but not seriously; his supporters take him seriously but not literally.**"[emphasis added]

Trump admitted by Twitter that his "use of social media is not Presidential—it's MODERN DAY PRESIDENTIAL. Make America Great Again!"

Hanson admits that Trump's timing was perfect. Obama virtually destroyed the Democrat Party that misconstrued his election as a "progressive mandate." Equality was no longer to be just legally protected. Since we are all racists, according to the liberal-left, equality has to be mandated.

Political Correctness sets the stage for a counter-attack, which mainstream Republicans (who claimed to be conservatives) were afraid to engage in because they wilted when accused of racism. Trump knows he is not a racist. His family, friends and business associates know he's not a racist. So he does not feel compelled to prove to his critics that he is not. He's already made billions of bucks.

What does Trump care what his leftist critics think? And his supporters loved it and we continue to love him for his willingness, in fact his zeal to fight back. Because we all know he's defending all of us who have been defamed and libeled for years by the left.

Obama told you that the government was responsible for your success. Trump said NO! Obama destroyed any semblance of a centrist Democrat politician. Trump picked up the pieces. While much is made of Clinton's popular vote majority, Hanson points out that her national margin "can be attributed to her California vote margin alone."

Hanson does not go very far in attributing that margin to illegal immigrant voting. But he goes into great and poignant detail as to how illegal immigration has virtually ruined the quiet farm community that he grew up in.

Unlike other Republican politicians who pander to the demands of illegal immigrants and their loud supporters, Trump unabashedly campaigned among people the most damaged by massive illegal immigration. Hanson points out that Republicans were fed up with a party that was "willing to repeatedly lose the presidency nobly."

THEME 6

THE ATTEMPTED COUP AGAINST THE PRESIDENT

REMEMBER WHEN THE LEFT accused the Nixon Administration of being an "imperial Presidency?" Hanson seems to have recognized Trump's greatest political challenge in office was a constant in great empires of the past. "All great empires of the past have produced 'deep states,'" writes Hanson. "The ancient Athenian Alcibiades supported every faction in Greece at one time or another, including Greece's historic enemy Persia.

Talleyrand was a fixture in the permanent Paris court from Monarchy to Revolution through Napoleon and the restored Monarchy spanning a period of forty years. His loyalty was always to Monsieur Talleyrand rather than to France."

In case you think his comparisons are far-fetched, consider these statistics from Hanson: "In America there are over 22 million federal, state and local employees, all dedicated to their own survival. The three largest labor unions represent government employees. In the Presidential election of 2016, 95% of all donations from federal workers went to Hillary Clinton. In 2020, federal workers again donated to Democrat Joe Biden in huge numbers."

Under Obama, the permanent bureaucracy or "Deep State" had been "thoroughly radicalized and emboldened, which explains why an anonymous senior level administration employee could say to the readers of the *New York Times* that his/

her colleagues were the true guardians of the nation's values and were doing whatever they could to remove Trump from office."

Emboldened deep-state careerists plotted against Trump—sometimes illegally and then lying about it under oath—include former CIA chief John Brennan, former DNI James Clapper, the fourth most senior official in the Justice Department Bruce Ohr, and former UN ambassador Samantha Power.

"There have been no legal consequences for them because they are protected by their friends who are still in government and who populate the media."

There is an interlocking directorate between major media figures, journalists, the deep-state apparatus, and the Clinton organization, often by marriage. Virtually every major media critic of Trump, including the social media moguls of Silicon Valley, has a profound and publicly undisclosed conflict of interest, according to Hanson.

Former CIA counter terrorism analyst Phil Mudd warned Jake Tapper in 2017 that **"the government is going to kill"** President Donald Trump [emphasis added]. The reason? **"Let me give you one bottom line as a former government official. The government is going to kill this guy. The government is going to kill this guy because he doesn't support them."** [emphasis added]

Hanson seems to be telling us that this kind of shocking, treasonous behavior should not shock us at all, considering the vast number of entrenched, permanent and very powerful people who work for the Federal Government and for a variety of reasons felt threatened by President Trump's very existence in office.

The full story of the attempted coup d'etat against President Trump has yet to be told, but by the time the 2020 election season was underway, his enemies had already conspired to remove him from office by impeaching him a second time and then rigging the election against him. A temporary setback for Trump's "America First" movement — we hope. But, regardless of the events of 2020's stolen election, most revealing is Hanson's treatment of the Mueller investigation.

He reveals the extent of deep state resistance, reaching back to early in the campaign during which Trump associates were surveilled and set up as a means of obtaining illegal FISA warrants to prove that Trump was being controlled and directed by Vladimir Putin. Even Obama made it clear that it was impossible to rig an American election.

There was real Russian collusion: between Christopher Steele, Fusion GPS and the Hillary Clinton campaign, with help from Comey's FBI and John Brennan at the CIA. Hanson firmly believes that Trump's inability to go much beyond 50% in popularity is due to the formidable forces arrayed against him.

Trump's enemies are the most formidable any President in history has ever faced.

Nonetheless, Trump's willingness to counter punch his critics and stand for the principles and policies mean there's a good chance his "America First" movement will continue to dominate American politics long into the future, starting with recapturing the House and Senate in 2022 and culminating with the election of another strong conservative president in 2024—maybe even Donald Trump himself!

Conclusion

Pick up the book, *The Case for Trump*. Hanson will enlighten, he will disturb, he will enrage, but he will also give you confidence that Donald Trump's "America First" vision is worth fighting for in 2022, 2024, and beyond. He will give you ammunition to respond to Trump's critics.

Try "Trump is a modern-day Thucydides" the next time your leftist neighbor (or brother-in-law) derides him as a fool and an idiot. Or the next time someone claims he's dangerous, just compare him to Truman.

Hanson, who appears on Fox TV regularly, is also a very good read. You will have the privilege of having a scholar's insights, but, like Trump, Hanson will never talk down to you. Nor ever abandon his conservative principles to share with you what he likes about Donald Trump. Get your hands on more of these pocketbooks to hand around to everyone you know as we work to elect pro-Trump conservatives to Congress in 2022 and send another "America First" conservative to the White House in 2024 (perhaps even Trump himself) and buy the Victor Hanson book, *The Case for Trump*. You can't lose.

AFTERWORD

By Fredy Burgos
Project Director, Americans for a Conservative Agenda
(formerly Americans for the Trump Agenda)

IF YOU READ THIS POCKETBOOK with an open mind, then you are most likely now, like us, fans of former President Donald Trump.

And if you started reading this pocketbook like us, already a Trump fan, then you will likely be very excited about this new tool to help undecided voters see what we love about former President Donald Trump.

If you want more of what you've read about in these pages, you need to say **TrumpYes**, right now. Help us.

First, you can give away your copy to a relative, friend, co-worker, neighbor or acquaintance who is open-minded about Donald Trump. This pocketbook is not for the haters.

You can order more copies of this pocketbook to give out. And you can donate to help us print and distribute more. Please. You can really help make the difference. America needs former President Trump to continue his leadership in the future and into the 2022 and 2024 elections. And we need you to help strengthen his voice.

And one more thing. Please consider purchasing the terrific book by Victor Davis Hanson by going to your nearby bookstore or visit FreedomPublishers.com, Barnes & Noble or Amazon.com. Thank you and God bless you.

THE WHITE HOUSE
WASHINGTON

October 25, 2018

Mr. Fredy Burgos
Stuarts Draft, Virginia

Dear Mr. Burgos,

Thank you for your kind letter and generous words of encouragement. Your unwavering faith and support sustain and inspire me in my efforts to strengthen and protect our Nation.

Since my first day in office, I have taken actions to keep Americans safe and restore the rule of law. Americans are living in communities that are safer, stronger, and more secure.

My Administration is making real change in Washington and creating a land of freedom and opportunity. Our Nation's economy is experiencing tremendous growth. Our country is roaring back more quickly than anyone could have predicted. From coast to coast, there is a renewed spirit of optimism, and the American Dream has never been more attainable.

Thank you again for your steadfast support. As President, I will continue to fight for and uphold the American values that you and I both cherish.

Sincerely,

[signature: Donald Trump]

TRUMP ACHIEVEMENTS

Before the China virus:
- Almost 4 million jobs created since election.
- New unemployment claims hit a 49-year low.
- Median household income hit highest level ever recorded.
- Signed the biggest package of tax cuts and reforms in history.
- Opened ANWR and approved Keystone XL and Dakota Access Pipelines.
- Record number of regulations eliminated.
- Obamacare individual mandate penalty GONE.
- Increased our coal exports by 60 percent; U.S. oil production reached all-time high.
- United States is a net natural gas exporter for the first time since 1957.
- Withdrew the United States from the job-killing Paris Climate Accord.
- Secured record $700 billion in military funding.
- Confirmed more Circuit Court judges than any other new administration.
- Confirmed Supreme Court Justice Neil Gorsuch and Judge Brett Kavanaugh.
- Withdrew from the horrible, one-sided Iran Deal.
- Moved U.S. Embassy to Jerusalem.
- Protecting Americans from terrorists with the Travel Ban, upheld by Supreme Court.
- Concluded a historic U.S.-Mexico Trade Deal to replace NAFTA.
- Imposed tariffs on China in response to China's forced technology transfer, intellectual property theft, and their chronically abusive trade practices.
- Improved vetting and screening for refugees, and switched focus to overseas resettlement.
- We began BUILDING THE WALL.

During the China virus:
- Acted fast to cut off travel from China and Europe or we would have had many, many more deaths.
- Led the way to re-open our economy; Meanwhile, Democrats fuel hysteria.
- Antifa designated a terrorist organization.
- Took tough action to make sure our nation's capital was safe from domestic terrorists.
- Continued building our big, beautiful border wall.